Gallop
Around The
GLOBE

Gallop
Around The
GLOBE

Ella Foxglove

Collins

Contents

Chapter 1 Europe: Gentle giants and
   dazzling dancers........................ 6

Bonus: Horse brasses..................... 22

Chapter 2 Asia: Heroic warriors and
   mountain couriers 24

Bonus: Horse markings 38

Chapter 3 North America: Spotty coats
   and musical riders 40

Bonus: Mounted police around
   the world................................ 54

Chapter 4 South America: Tiny helpers
   and cowboy companions 56

Bonus: Cowboys around the world 72

Chapter 5 Oceania: Wild runners and
    hard workers............................ 74

Bonus: Horse timeline.................... 88

Chapter 6 Africa: Desert travellers
    and rugged racers 90

Bonus: Horses around the world.......... 104

About the author 106

Book chat 108

CHAPTER 1
Europe: Gentle giants and dazzling dancers

The stupendous Shire horse

Gentle giants

Shire horses are known as 'gentle giants' due to their impressive size and their calm and friendly personalities.

For thousands of years, people have used horses to help carry heavy loads. To make the horses more efficient, farmers bred them to be bigger and stronger.

In the UK, those big horses were carefully bred until they became the most enormous horses of all – the Shire horses.

Unlike humans, horses are measured for height to the tops of their shoulders (called withers). This is because horses move their heads up and down a lot, so measuring to the top of their head wouldn't be consistent or accurate!

Fact
The biggest horse that ever lived was Sampson, a Shire horse born in 1846. He was 219 centimetres tall and weighed 1,524 kilograms. That's as heavy as a hippopotamus!

Hard-working horses

Shire horses can work really hard, which is lucky, because 200 years ago, they were essential to farming, trade and transport.

Some Shire horses worked on farms, pulling ploughs to get the soil ready for planting new crops. Later in the year, they pulled reaping machines to gather in the harvest.

Others pulled narrowboats, transporting important supplies like coal and timber along canals. This could be dangerous: if a horse fell in the water, they might not be able to climb out again.

Shire horses also made local deliveries, pulling heavy kegs on a flat cart called a dray. Shire horses can pull up to four tonnes in weight – that's like pulling an elephant!

The end of the Shires?

In the 1800s, there were roughly ten million people living in the UK – and over a million Shire horses. So, for every ten people, there was one Shire horse! That isn't the case today, so where did they go?

With the invention of modern machinery like tractors and lorries, the need for Shire horses diminished.

Fact
Tractors can plough 30 times faster than horses!

Today, there are only around 1,500 Shire horses left. Most live at visitor centres where people can learn more about them.

The Shire Horse Society is committed to ensuring that this wonderful breed of gentle giants continues to thrive.

Case study: Shires today

Location: Hook Norton, Oxfordshire, England

Today, most companies use lorries for deliveries, but if you visit Hook Norton in Oxfordshire, you'll still see Shire horses, pulling a dray just like their ancestors did.

The Shire horses of Hook Norton are called Brigadier, Balmoral and Cromwell. Cromwell is the youngest and he's very inquisitive!

On delivery days, the driver starts by tacking up the horses, which means putting on their harness and bridle. When the kegs are loaded onto the dray, it's time to set off. Once they arrive, the horses wait while the kegs are unloaded and might enjoy a carrot snack. Then it's off to the next stop.

When the last delivery is finished, Brigadier, Balmoral and Cromwell take a break. They have their own stables and 18 acres of beautiful countryside to roam.

The leaping Lipizzaner

Dancing horses

Dressage is an equestrian sport where horses work in harmony with their riders to perform different movements, often in time to music. Learning dressage makes horses more flexible and keeps them healthy too – dressage is like a dance class for them!

Any kind of horse can learn dressage, but Lipizzaners are the only breed to perform at the Spanish Riding School, the oldest dressage school in the world. People come from all over the world to see them dance.

Most Lipizzaners have white coats, but we call them 'grey'. Grey horses have white coats and black skin, while white horses have white coats and pink skin. Look at their noses: if you see a black nose, it's a grey horse!

Fact
The Spanish Riding School is in Vienna, Austria – not Spain!

Dancing on air

What does horse dancing look like? Well, there are lots of different movements and it takes a long time to learn them all. After many years at the riding school, the Lipizzaners are ready to perform the most difficult movements of all: special jumps called 'airs above the ground'.

Here are some of the main movements.

The passage (a trot with the legs lifted high).

The courbette (a hop on the back legs).

The levade (a rearing pose).

The capriole (a leap with a kick of the back legs).

Hannah Zeitlhofer

For hundreds of years, only men rode the Lipizzaners at the Spanish Riding School. That changed in 2008, when the school's new director encouraged female riders to apply.

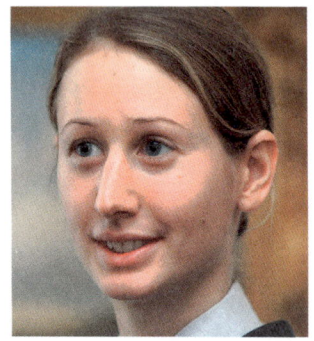

Hannah Zeitlhofer was determined to get in. She'd always loved dressage and had even studied Equestrian Science, the science of horses, at university.

After a tough audition where Hannah had to demonstrate her dressage skills in front of the school's experts, she got the good news: she'd been accepted!

In 2016, Hannah finished training and became the first female rider at the school. Now she also teaches new students – of any gender.

Operation Cowboy

If it weren't for the actions of one brave man, there might not be any Lipizzaners left today.

During the Second World War, the German government wanted to breed more Lipizzaners and not share them with any other country. They sent soldiers to transport the Lipizzaner mares away from the Riding School and hide them near a small town called Hostau. At first, the Lipizzaner mares and their foals were safe, but in 1945, the Soviet army started marching towards Hostau. What if there was a battle and the Lipizzaners got hurt?

Alois Podhajsky

Alois Podhajsky was the head of the Riding School and he knew it was his job to protect the Lipizzaners. He contacted the American army, and together they made a rescue plan called 'Operation Cowboy'.

The American soldiers sneaked into the countryside and loaded the Lipizzaner mares and their foals into trucks, driving them to safety.

Bonus
Horse brasses

A horse brass is a type of decoration worn by Shire horses. Think of them as horse jewellery! They're brass circles attached to the horse's harness and each one has a shape or picture in the middle.

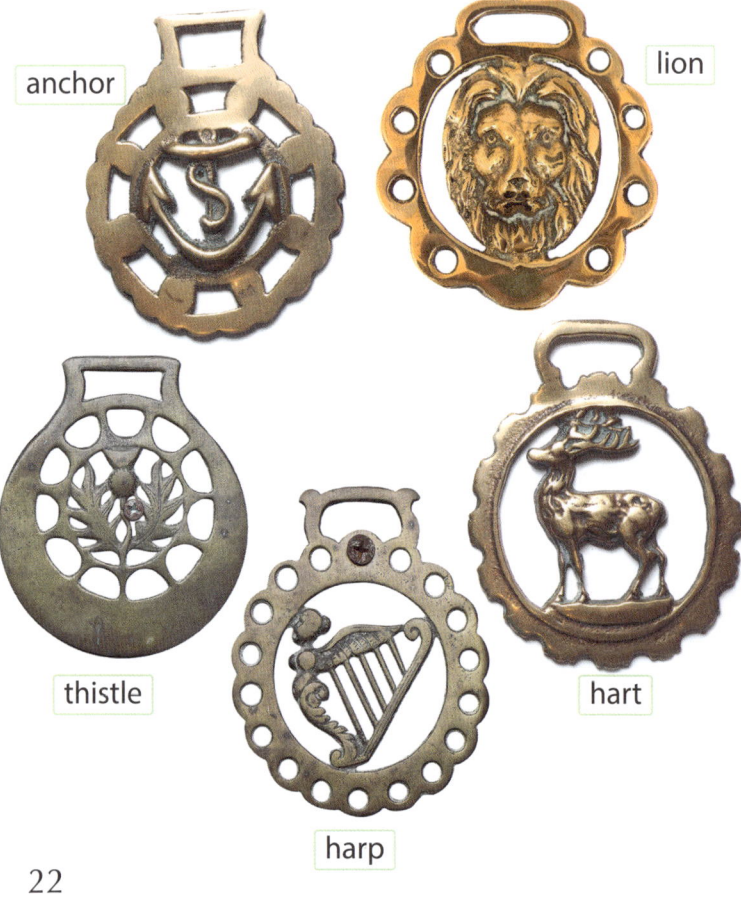

anchor

lion

thistle

harp

hart

CHAPTER 2
Asia: Heroic warriors and mountain couriers

The magical Marwari horse

Divine beings

Marwari horses are easy to spot, thanks to their banana-shaped ears that meet in the middle. They've also been around for over 800 years! Back in the 12th century, the rulers of the Marwar region of India started breeding horses for war, making them even braver and tougher.

People were so impressed by the horses' bravery that, at that time, they thought they must be divine beings. Because of this, only certain families and warriors were allowed to ride them.

Today, there are around 3,000 Marwari horses left in the world, and you can only see them if you visit India. The Indian government wants to protect the Marwari horses and their culture by keeping them together, so no one is allowed to take Marwari horses out of the country.

a painting of Emperor Shah Jahan I riding his favourite horse in 1630

Marwaris in battle

One of the earliest stories about these brave Indian warhorses is the story of Chetak, who was wounded in battle in 1576 but still carried his rider to safety. There are several statues of Chetak in India to commemorate his loyalty and courage.

Jodhpurs

Indian soldiers in the Jodhpur region wore tight trousers with tough fabric on the inside of the legs to protect them from rubbing against the saddle. When a ruler of Jodhpur visited England in 1897, he started a new trend! Jodhpur trousers are still worn by many riders today.

> **Fact**
> Indian soldiers rode elephants and camels as well as horses.

A memorial in New Delhi, India, commemorates the bravery of the Jodhpur Lancers and their horses.

The last battle

The last time anyone rode Marwari horses into battle was during the First World War, in 1918. A group of Indian soldiers called the Jodhpur Lancers rode Marwari horses when they fought to liberate the town of Haifa from the Ottoman and German armies. Despite being outnumbered, the Marwari horses charged courageously to the town's defence.

The saviour of the Marwari

Just over 100 years ago, it looked as if Marwari horses might become extinct.

One man, Umaid Singh, saved these incredible horses from extinction. He wanted to keep the breed alive and continue his family's connection to the Marwari. When he became the ruler of Jodhpur, he knew exactly what to do.

Umaid bought lots of Marwari horses and started breeding them to increase the population. Today, the Marwari Horse Society works to carry on Umaid's legacy and protect Marwari horses all over India.

Umaid Singh ruled Jodhpur from 1918 to 1947.

Marwari mare wearing traditional tack and saddle

The tough Tibetan pony

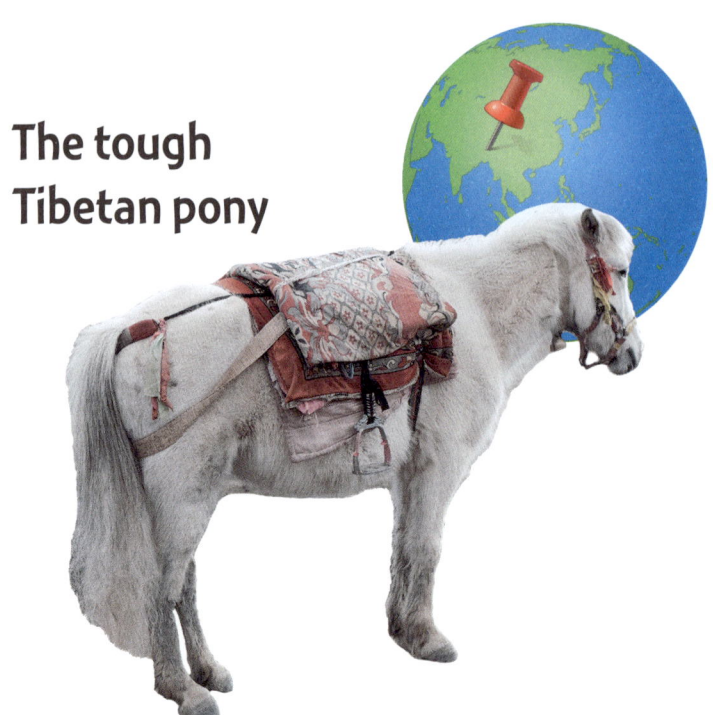

Mountain survival

Tibetan ponies are an important part of life in Tibet. Tibet is mountainous, so people need sure-footed ponies to travel up steep and twisting tracks where cars aren't able to go. But why are Tibetan ponies so good at surviving in the mountains?

Though Tibetan ponies are small, they're extremely tough. They can also climb! A Tibetan pony can travel up a steep mountain path without falling – even with a person on its back!

How do you travel safely through dangerous snowy mountains? You take a Tibetan pony.

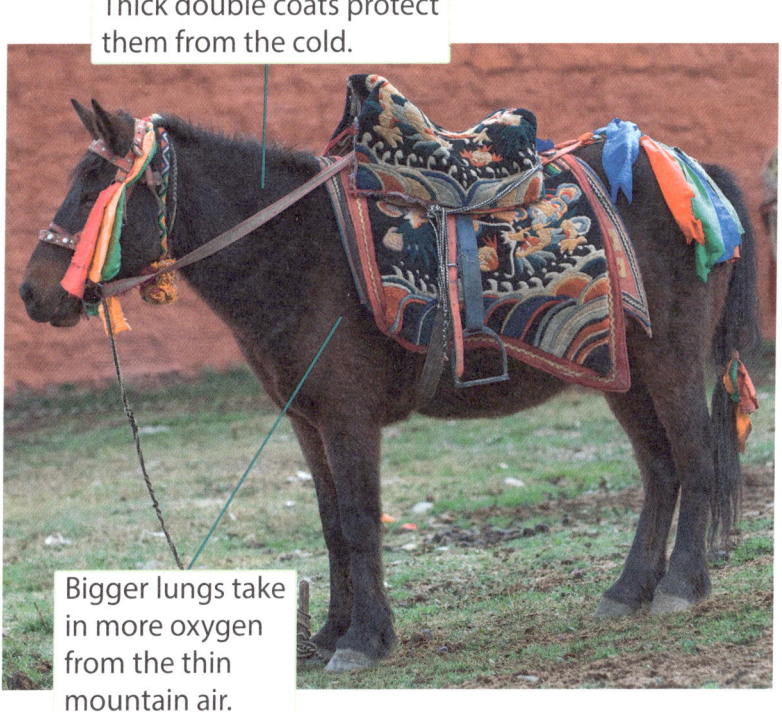

Thick double coats protect them from the cold.

Bigger lungs take in more oxygen from the thin mountain air.

The Tea Horse Road

Starting in the 6th century, Tibetan ponies carried tea along the Tea Horse Road. The harsh environment meant the journey was dangerous, and only Tibetan ponies were able to climb the steep paths carrying heavy loads; without them, there was no way to transport the tea.

The ponies formed close bonds with the traders who owned them, because they had to rely on each other for survival. Together, they fought through snowstorms, avalanches, and attacks by predators to deliver their valuable cargo.

For 1,400 years, Tibetan ponies brought tea via the Tea Horse Road. The tea then travelled from Tibet to Europe, so the Tea Horse Road is the reason there's tea in Europe today!

Fact

The Tea Horse Road was part of the longest trade route in history.

The Litang Horse Festival

The Khampas are a nomadic people who travel from place to place and usually herd yak, cattle and goats, but every August they converge on the Tibetan Plateau and set up their tents, ready to celebrate the Litang Horse Festival.

The festival is extremely popular. Tourists from around the world attend to watch the Khampas and their ponies race. The riders wear bright robes and shirts, while the ponies wear colourful nosebands and blankets.

Riders and their ponies practise running before races.

While the races are going on, people cheer and participate in group dances. The festival is a way for everyone to come together and celebrate Tibetan ponies and traditional Tibetan culture.

Fact
The Tibetan Pony Initiative was set up in 2023 to ensure that sick and injured ponies in remote areas still receive medical treatment.

The Epic of King Gesar

There's a famous story in Tibet about a king called Gesar and his best friend, the magical horse Kyang Go Karkar.

When Gesar was only 12 years old, there was a competition to decide who would become king. All the other racers were much older than Gesar and no one thought he could win. Luckily, the magical horse Kyang Go Karkar left the mountains to come and help him.

King Gesar riding Kyang Go Karkar

Kyang Go Karkar wasn't just the fastest horse in the world – he could fly. The other horses didn't stand a chance! Gesar and Kyang Go Karkar raced ahead and crossed the finish line, and Gesar became king. He and Kyang Go Karkar went on to have lots of adventures together.

> **Fact**
> There are lots more stories about Gesar in a long poem called *The Epic of King Gesar*.

a statue of Gesar and Kyang Go Karkar in Tibet

Bonus
Horse markings

Every horse has its own markings and they all have special names.

Star: white mark on forehead

Stripe: thin white line down nose

Blaze: wide white line down nose

Snip: white mark on nose

Coronet: white around the top of the hoof

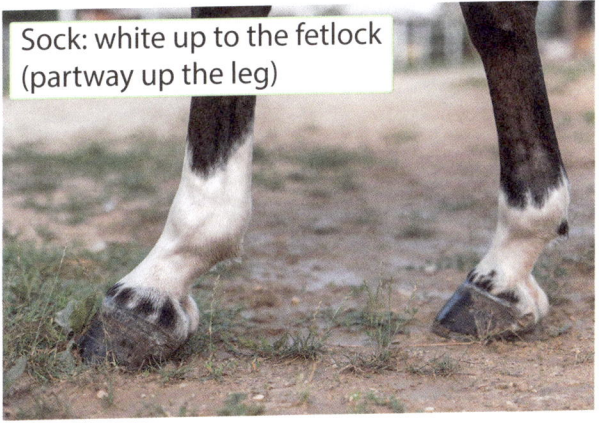

Sock: white up to the fetlock (partway up the leg)

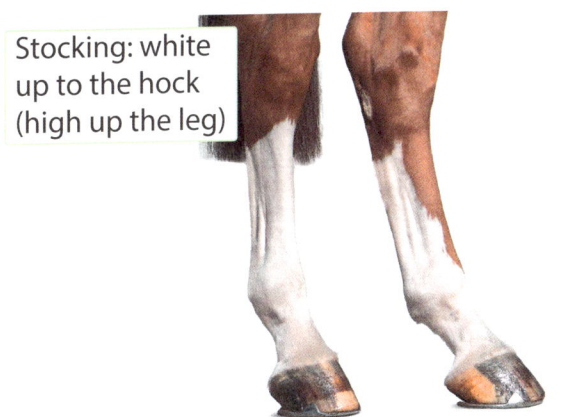

Stocking: white up to the hock (high up the leg)

CHAPTER 3
North America: Spotty coats and musical riders

The affable Appaloosa

Ancient Appaloosas

Appaloosa horses are known for their spotted coats. Spotted horses have been around for thousands of years – they even appear in prehistoric cave paintings in Europe!

Hundreds of years ago, there were no horses in North America, but when Europeans travelled across the Atlantic Ocean they brought horses with them. Soon there were horses living all over North America. The indigenous tribes of North America quickly saw how useful horses could be, so they began keeping horses of their own. Horses were useful for travelling long distances swiftly, and hunting animals such as deer and bison.

The Nez Perce Tribe of North America started breeding their own horses in the 1750s. A century later, the Nez Perce horses were extremely popular thanks to their strength and elegance. Everyone wanted a Nez Perce horse!

The Nez Perce bred more and more foals with spotty coats, until they evolved into the breed we now call the Appaloosa.

Fact
The name Appaloosa comes from the Palouse River which runs through Nez Perce tribal lands.

Not just spots

Different Appaloosas have different spot patterns. Some only have spots on their back, while others are spotty all over.

leopard

blanket

snowflake

The type of pattern an Appaloosa has depends on the genes it inherits from its parents. Some Appaloosas lack the so-called 'leopard gene' that results in a spotty coat. These Appaloosas don't have any spots at all.

It isn't just their coats that make Appaloosas unique. If you want to identify an Appaloosa, you should also look out for some of these signs.

thin mane

white around the eyes

stripy hooves

Moon blindness

On rare occasions, horses can develop an incurable condition called moon blindness that causes painful eye infections. Sometimes the best way to help the horse feel better is to remove their eyes.

There are lots of blind and partially sighted horses around the world – and many are Appaloosas. With love and support, they can live long and happy lives.

Blind Appaloosa heroes

Endo in Oregon holds the world record for the highest jump made by a blind horse. Jumping is his favourite activity!

Another Appaloosa, Ward, who lives in Florida, is best friends with a donkey named Poppi who leads him around like a guide dog!

Valentino in California was a police horse until he lost an eye. Now he's retired and spends his days eating apples!

Fact
Appaloosas are eight times more likely than other horses to get moon blindness.

The Appaloosa registry

In 1877, the Nez Perce Tribe fought a war to defend their ancestral lands. Many people and horses were killed in the conflict, and for decades there were only a few Appaloosa horses left.

To save the breed from extinction, a man named Claude Thompson started a registry, a list of Appaloosas that made it easier for their owners to find each other and breed their horses together.

The registry started with only 200 horses, but swiftly grew. Today there are more than 635,000 horses listed in the Appaloosa registry!

Fact
1 in 50 horses in the US are Appaloosas!

The helpful Hanoverian

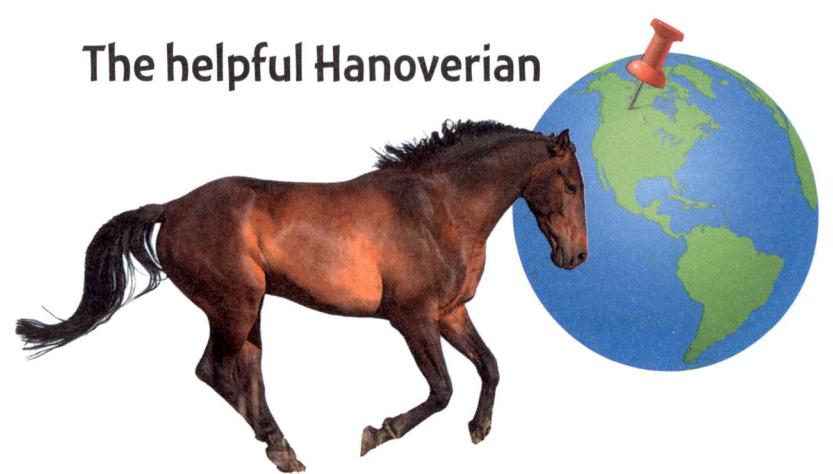

For 300 years, Hanoverian horses have helped people with all kinds of jobs. They've worked in the army and on farms, and have taken part in riding competitions. Some Hanoverians have competed in the Olympics and won medals. Whatever you need a horse for, a Hanoverian can help.

The first Hanoverians came from Germany, but they can now be found all over the world. Some of the most famous Hanoverians live in Canada and work for the Canadian police.

Warmbloods, coldbloods and hotbloods

We sometimes sort horse breeds into three groups based on body types and personalities. The groups aren't actually anything to do with the horses' blood, though. They're just names!

Spot a coldblood
– heavy build
– feathers (long hair) on legs
– calm and gentle

Spot a warmblood
– muscular build
– high withers (shoulders)
– versatile and athletic

Spot a hotblood
– light build
– tail held high
– quick and energetic

Fact
Hanoverians are warmblood horses! Thanks to their strength and flexibility, they're good at lots of different equestrian sports like dressage and showjumping.

Musical Ride

Royal Canadian Mounted Police are called 'Mounties' because they used to be 'mounted' on horses for daily patrols. Over a hundred years ago, they held a uniformed parade to show off their skills and started a new tradition. They began holding regular parades across the country, all of them set to music, and the parade was named the Musical Ride.

In the 1930s, the Mounties stopped using horses for police work, but they decided to keep up the Musical Ride tradition. Today, there are 32 horses and riders who keep the tradition of the Musical Ride's uniformed parades going strong.

The Musical Ride horses are so famous, there's a competition every year in Canada to name the new foals.

The Musical Ride is a special unit of mounted police who put on horse-riding displays across Canada.

The Royal Hanoverians

The Musical Ride stables are in Ottawa, Canada.

The Musical Ride Hanoverians in Canada have a special relationship with the British Royal family. In 1969, the Canadian police gave Queen Elizabeth II a Hanoverian named Burmese. He quickly became her favourite horse.

Queen Elizabeth II riding Burmese in 1982

Thanks to Burmese, the Canadian police and the Royal family still have a tradition of giving each other horses as gifts. In 2018, the Royal family gave the Canadian police a Hanoverian named Victoria.

Victoria is now part of the Musical Ride and lives in Canada. Every morning, the riders groom her coat until it shines, and afterwards she munches on a hay breakfast while they sweep out the stables and tidy up. Then it's time to go riding! Victoria and the other horses practise for the parade, when they'll be able to show off their skills.

> **Fact**
> The Canadian police also gave King Charles III a Hanoverian named Noble. The King rides Noble during parades.

Bonus
Mounted police around the world

It's not just Royal Canadian Mounted Police who own horses. There are lots of mounted police around the world and many of them still ride horses at work.

Canada – Royal Canadian Mounted Police

US – New York City Police Department Mounted Unit

UK – Metropolitan Police Mounted Branch

China – Mounted Policewomen Unit

India – Kolkata Mounted Police

Australia – New South Wales Mounted Police

South Africa – South African Police Service Mounted Units

CHAPTER 4
South America: Tiny helpers and cowboy companions

The friendly Falabella

The Falabella is the smallest horse in the world. But how did it get that way?

In the 19th century, people noticed that some of the horses living wild in Argentina were smaller than average. Two men named Patrick Newtail and Juan Falabella captured some of the horses and began breeding them to make them even smaller.

Patrick and Juan wanted small, friendly horses – and that's exactly what they got. The new breed was named Falabella after Juan's surname, and they were all under 76 centimetres tall. That's the same size as a large dog!

Not everything about Falabellas is small. They have the same-sized hearts as bigger horse breeds, and some people think that's why they live such a long time – up to 40 years!

Fact
Falabellas have fewer bones in their spine than other horses.

Horse or pony?

Even though Falabellas are small, we call them miniature horses and not ponies. How can we tell the difference?

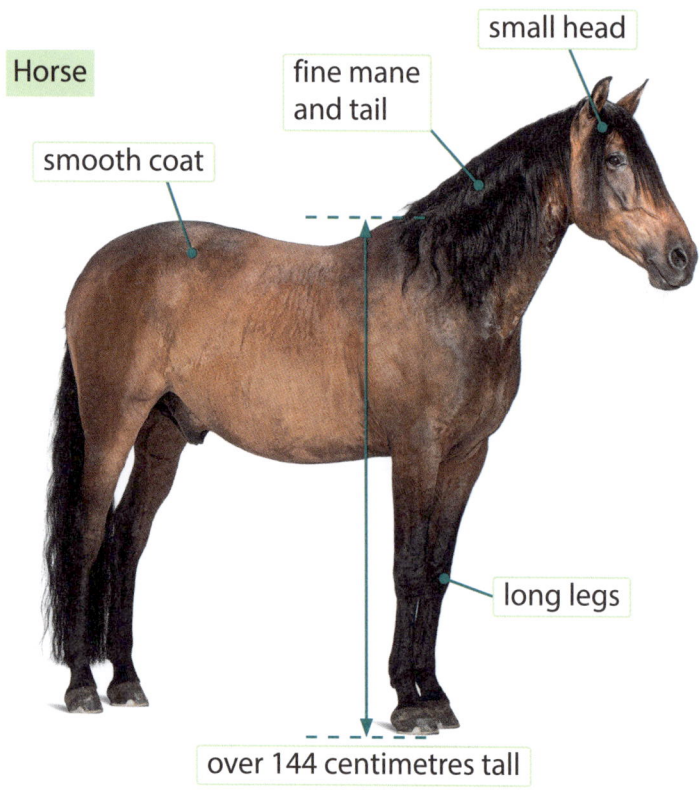

Horse

- small head
- fine mane and tail
- smooth coat
- long legs
- over 144 centimetres tall

Pony

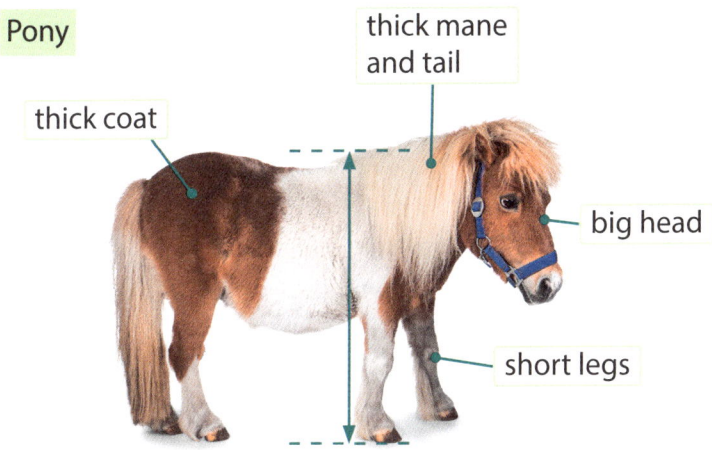

- thick coat
- thick mane and tail
- big head
- short legs
- under 144 centimetres tall

Miniature horse

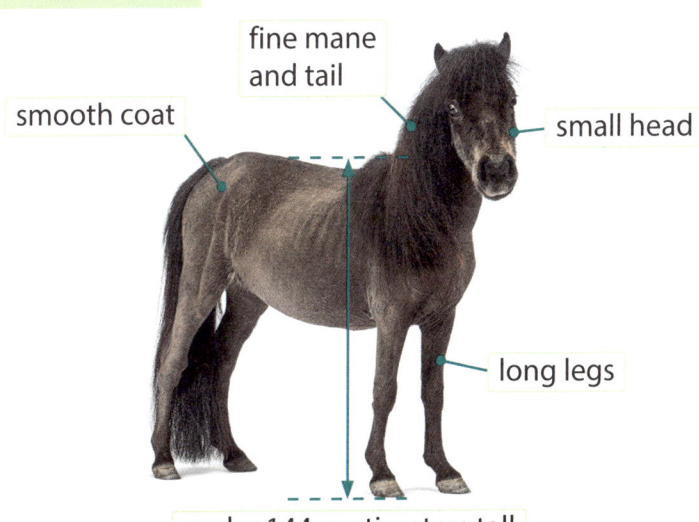

- smooth coat
- fine mane and tail
- small head
- long legs
- under 144 centimetres tall

Lord and Lady Fisher's Falabellas

For a long time, Falabella horses only lived in Argentina. Then, in 1977, a couple named Lord and Lady Fisher visited Argentina and asked if they could bring some Falabella horses to the UK. The Fishers had turned their family estate into a wildlife park and could give the horses a good home. The Falabella family agreed that Lord and Lady Fisher would be allowed to breed Falabella horses in the UK.

Lord and Lady Fisher's Falabellas were sometimes allowed inside the house.

Lord and Lady Fisher wanted to share the friendly Falabellas with everyone. Visitors to the wildlife park were astounded! Such tiny horses had never been seen in the UK, and the Falabellas swiftly became the park's most popular attraction.

Thanks to Lord and Lady Fisher, the Falabellas became famous and more people started breeding them. Now there are Falabellas all around the world.

Case study: Therapy ponies

Charity: Therapy Ponies Scotland

Horse: Bentley the Falabella

Therapy ponies visit people in places like care homes or hospitals to help improve their mental and emotional wellbeing. Interacting with friendly animals causes our bodies to release oxytocin, a chemical that reduces stress and make us feel safe and relaxed.

Therapy Ponies Scotland owns 13 ponies – and one miniature horse! Bentley the Fallabella's small size and friendly personality mean he's perfect for the job.

It's not often you see a horse indoors, but Bentley makes himself at home. He stands patiently and enjoys getting his ears scratched and his nose rubbed. Both Bentley and the people he visits get a lot out of the visit.

Fact

Therapy ponies wear boots to protect their hooves indoors.

The clever Criollo

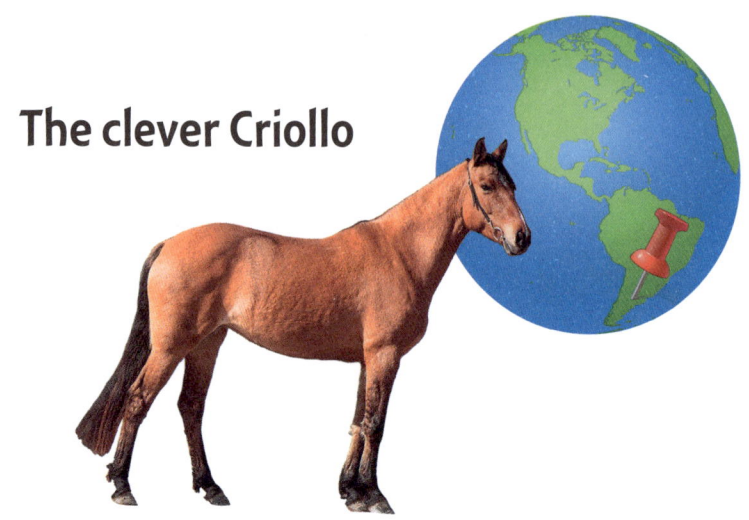

Over 400 years ago, Spanish people brought horses to the Pampas plains in South America, and some of the horses escaped and began living in the wild. Over time, they evolved to survive on dry grass and minimal water. These horses were the ancestors of the modern Criollo horses.

Fact
The Pampas plains of South America cover a larger area than the whole of the UK.

The cowboy horse

Gauchos are cowboys who live and work in Argentina and other South American countries. They often ride Criollo horses because these horses are good at herding other animals and can travel all day carrying heavy loads. Criollo horses are also a symbol of independence and survival in tough conditions, which is an important part of South American culture.

Cow sense

Criollo horses also have a special skill called cow sense. Horses with cow sense are excellent herders, because they understand cow behaviour.

Sometimes gauchos need to separate a cow from the rest of the herd because it needs medical treatment or it's going to be sold. That's where the Criollo horse comes in!

The gaucho rides after the cow and catches it by throwing a lasso – a rope with a loop at one end. After tying the end of the rope to the front of the saddle, the gaucho and their Criollo can lead the cow away.

A three year ride!

In 1925, a man named Aimé Tschiffely decided to ride two Criollos named Mancha and Gato from Argentina to the US. Together, they travelled 16,000 kilometres across mountains, jungles and deserts. Their journey took three whole years!

Fact
Mancha means 'spot' and *gato* means 'cat'.

Aimé wrote a book about travelling with Mancha and Gato. He said Mancha was best at looking ahead to see what was on the horizon, while Gato had a talent for finding safe paths through bogs and mud. Every morning, both horses would greet him with a nicker, a friendly sound that horses make to say hello.

Aimé never forgot the two loyal Criollos. After he died, his ashes were buried next to Mancha and Gato so the three of them could be together forever.

Pleasure riding

Riding a horse for fun is called pleasure riding. Pleasure riding can happen inside an enclosed area like a field or out in the countryside. Sometimes you'll even spot horses and riders walking down the road beside the cars!

Riding for pleasure is relaxing for lots of people. Riders and their horses travel through the landscape together, soaking up the scenery and keeping each other company. It's a way to feel closer to nature.

In both North and South America, it's a popular tourist activity to book a day's pleasure riding on Criollo horses led by a guide. Criollos are used to walking over uneven terrain and don't get nervous, so they're perfect for exploring new places.

> **Fact**
> A horse who's only ridden for pleasure is called a hack. Riding outside for pleasure is also called 'going on a hack'.

Bonus
Cowboys around the world

People who ride horses to herd other animals such as sheep and cows are called 'cowboys' in the US but have different names around the world.

Argentina – gaucho

US – cowboy

Australia – stockman

Mexico – vaquero

France – gardian

Italy – buttero

Hungary – csikós

CHAPTER 5
Oceania: Wild runners and hard workers

The bold Brumby

In 1788, a group of ships set sail from England, carrying 1,400 people and seven horses halfway around the world to Australia. The journey took over eight months!

The horses lived in their own rooms under the ship's deck, and some horses had cloth slings under their bellies to help them stay on their feet as the waves moved the ship back and forth.

Many people from the UK began emigrating to Australia, and more and more ships filled with people and horses kept arriving.

Some of the horses escaped and learned to survive independently. Their descendants became the Brumbies.

Does this mean Brumbies are wild horses? Not exactly. Brumbies are feral, which means that they live in the wild, but they're descended from domesticated animals who lived alongside humans. In fact, lots of people catch Brumbies and teach them to trust humans so they can be ridden.

First Nation Australian stockwomen

Australians who ride horses to help herd cows and sheep are called stockmen and stockwomen.

The European settlers who arrived in Australia were prejudiced against First Nation Australians, whose ancestors had lived in Australia for thousands of years. They passed unfair laws that took away their land and separated their families. They also passed a law that First Nation Australian women weren't allowed to ride Brumbies and work as stockwomen. To defy the unfair law, some women carried on working in secret or disguised themselves as men.

After many years, the law changed, and now First Nation Australian women can be stockwomen, working alongside men.

First Nation Australian stockwomen from the 1900s

Brumbies and the environment

Brumbies spend 17 hours a day eating.

Brumbies are an important part of Australian history and culture, but they aren't native to Australia. They're also big animals that trample fragile soil and eat lots of plants. This damages the environment and makes it harder for other animals to survive.

Lots of Australians love the Brumbies, but they also want to take care of the environment. Some people think it's a good idea to reduce the number of Brumbies, while others want to move them to places where they won't cause any damage.

There are lots of different organisations in Australia that are working hard to protect Brumbies and help them live in harmony with the environment.

Case study: New homes for Brumbies

Charity: The Brumby Project

Brumby rescuer: Anna Uhrig

Anna Uhrig is an ecologist who studies the environment. She also loves Brumbies! She decided to help the Brumbies and protect the environment in Australia by founding The Brumby Project, which rescues Brumbies from the wild and finds them new homes. This protects them from people who might kill them to reduce the number of Brumbies in the wild.

When new Brumbies arrive at The Brumby Project, they've never been ridden before, so Anna teaches them how to wear a saddle and bridle and let someone sit on their back. It's important to be patient and kind with the Brumbies while they learn, because they're not used to being around people. However, Anna says teaching horses is sometimes easier than teaching people!

Before long, the Brumbies are saddled up and taking part in Brumby camps where horses and their riders bond with each other by training together. Soon, they'll be ready to go to their new homes.

Fact
Teaching a horse to let someone ride them is called 'breaking in'. It's more gentle than it sounds!

The mighty Marquesas horse

The Marquesas Islands are in the middle of the Pacific Ocean, so how did horses get there and when did they arrive? We're not sure, but we do know that the Polynesians who live on the Marquesas Islands have a very special relationship with their horses.

Marquesas horses aren't just used for riding and farm work – they're a symbol of strength and independence. Several festivals take place throughout the year where people celebrate traditional Marquesas Islands culture with horse races and rodeos to show off their skills.

Most Marquesas horses roam freely when they're not being ridden.

Special saddles

The Marquesas horses wear saddles made of wood!

The Marquesas islanders carve the saddle into the perfect shape, and underneath they use pads made of sackcloth or colourful material to protect the horse's skin.

Wood carving is one of the islands' most ancient traditions, and wood carvers are called 'tuhuna'. Tuhuna carve saddles, sculptures, bowls – anything they can think of! These beautiful works of art are handcrafted and completely unique. That means no two Marquesas horses wear the same saddle! They all have different patterns and designs carved on them.

Inspiring art and literature

Many people have been inspired by Marquesas horses.

Paul Gauguin was a French artist and sculptor who lived on the Marquesas Islands over a hundred years ago. Lots of his paintings featured Marquesas horses.

Robert Louis Stevenson was a Scottish poet and writer who visited the islands in the 19th century. He wrote a book about the islands, including his adventures riding horses in the mountains.

Riders on the Beach by Paul Gauguin, 1902

Fact

Robert Louis Stevenson also wrote the famous pirate story *Treasure Island*.

Case study: Horse trainers

Location: Ua Huka (one of the Marquesas Islands)

Rider: Vohi Brown (horse trainer)

Vohi is the best horse trainer on the Marquesas Islands, and sometimes he takes tourists on riding tours to see the lush forests and sandy beaches where herds of horses run free.

After a long day of riding, Vohi cooks dinner in a traditional earth oven called an umu, while the horses munch on their favourite breadfruit leaves and take a well-earned rest.

Vohi also helps young horses learn to trust humans by speaking to them quietly and stroking them gently. He teaches his skills to the younger generation to help keep their cultural traditions alive.

Fact
Vohi loves the Marquesas horses so much he has one tattooed on his back!

A trainer takes his horse for a soothing walk in the waves.

Bonus
Horse timeline

Did you know horses have existed for over 50 million years? They used to look very different.

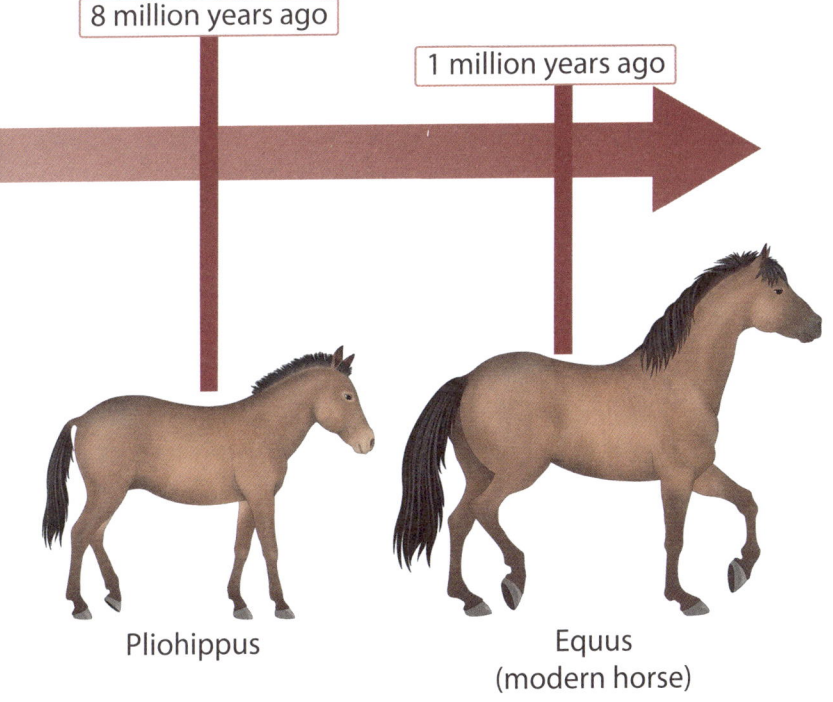

CHAPTER 6
Africa: Desert travellers and rugged racers

The adaptable Arabian

The Bedouin people are nomads who live in Africa and Arabia, and they were some of the first people in the world to breed horses. The Bedouin bred horses that could carry them even in the burning heat of the desert.

Domestic horses used to be wild animals, but over thousands of years they learned to trust humans and work with us.

Some of the first horses to become domestic animals were Arabians, and thanks to their survival skills and adaptability, there are now more than one million Arabian horses all over the world.

The Arabian breed is around 5,000 years old and there are different stories about its origins. The most famous story is the legend of Al Khamsa, a group of five mares who were so loyal they ran back to their owner when he called them away from an oasis filled with water. The legend says that all Arabian horses are descended from these five mares.

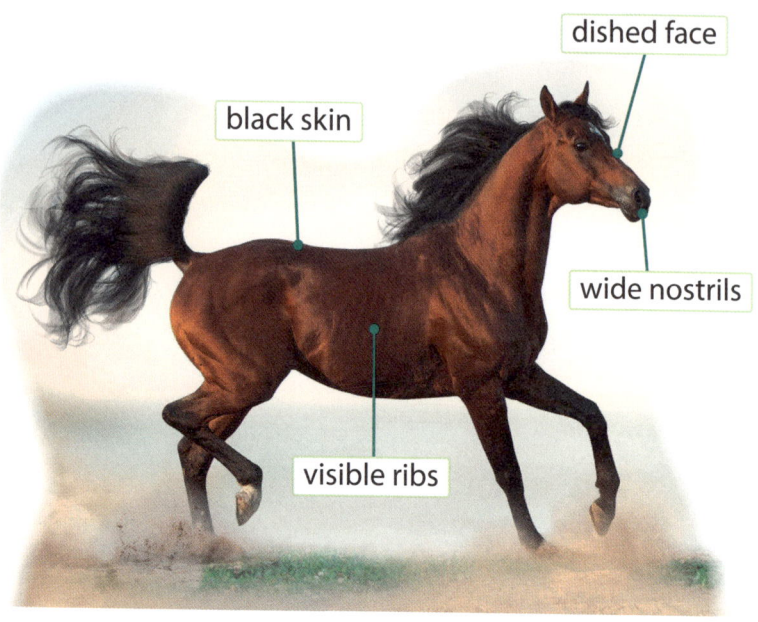

Arabian horses have adapted to survive in the harsh and dangerous desert. Their big rib cages and concave faces with wide nostrils help them breathe more deeply and efficiently when running all day across the sand. Underneath their coats, they have black skin that helps protect them from the sun. Black skin contains more melanin, which helps prevent cells from being damaged by the sun's rays.

We say that Arabian horses have 'dished' faces because their noses are concave like a dish.

> **Fact**
> Arabian horses can travel up to 160 kilometres a day.

In Arabian poetry, Arabian horses are called 'drinkers of the wind and swallowers of the ground' because they breathe very deeply and can run a long way.

The Emperor's horse

Marengo the Arabian horse lived over two centuries ago and is one of the most famous warhorses in history. He was born in Egypt, but when he was six years old, Napoleon, the Emperor of France, was visiting and decided to buy him.

This painting is called *Napoleon Crossing the Alps* and the horse is believed to be Marengo.

Marengo travelled all the way from Egypt to France and became Napoleon's favourite warhorse.

In 1815, Marengo was captured by a British soldier and taken to England, where he lived for the rest of his life. Marengo lived until he was 38 years old. That's like a human living to 105!

Marengo's skeleton is in the National Army Museum in London.

Fact

If you ever visit Marengo, make sure to count his rib bones! Most horses have 18 pairs of ribs, but Arabians only have 17.

Endurance races

The Bedouin people still keep Arabian horses. They hold cultural festivals that celebrate traditional music and art.

These festivals also have horse races which are over short distances, but Arabians excel in long distance races, called endurance races, that are held all over the world.

The longest endurance race in the world takes place in Australia, and it's named after a famous Arabian horse named Shahzada. The Shahzada race is over 400 kilometres long and takes five days to complete!

Shahzada the Arabian horse won two 480-kilometre races.

The brave Basotho pony

Basotho ponies live in the mountainous country of Lesotho, and they come with their own hiking boots! Basotho ponies are descended from the horses that Dutch people brought to South Africa almost 400 years ago. Basotho ponies have tough hooves to protect their feet from the rocky terrain.

The Basotho pony was so popular that people started breeding them with other horses. Many of the new foals were born without the special Basotho pony characteristics and the breed started to disappear.

By the 1970s, there weren't many Basotho ponies left, and the Basotho Pony Project began in Lesotho, to breed more ponies and look after them. The project worked, and the Basotho ponies were saved from extinction.

Today, there are still some people in Lesotho who live high up in the mountains and ride Basotho ponies to get around.

Even though Basotho ponies have tough hooves, it's still important to look after their feet, because if their hooves get damaged, they won't be able to walk.

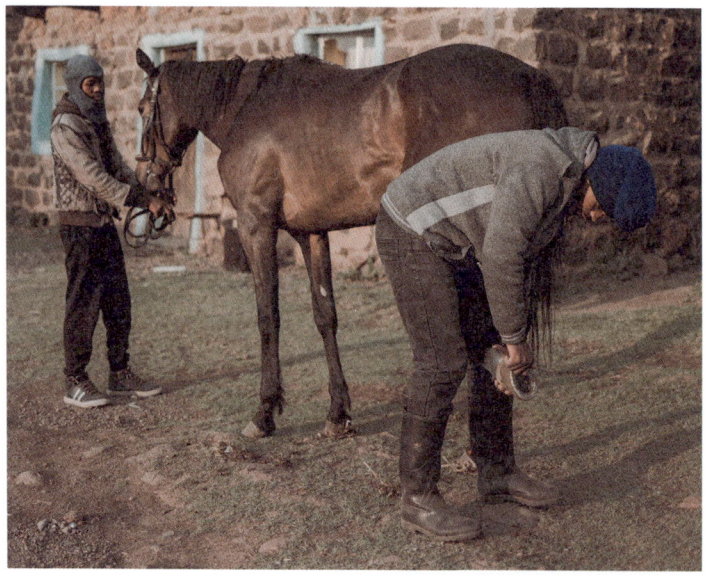

Have you ever had shoes that didn't fit properly? It's not very comfortable. Horses need shoes that fit properly too. People who look after horses' hooves and fit their shoes are called farriers.

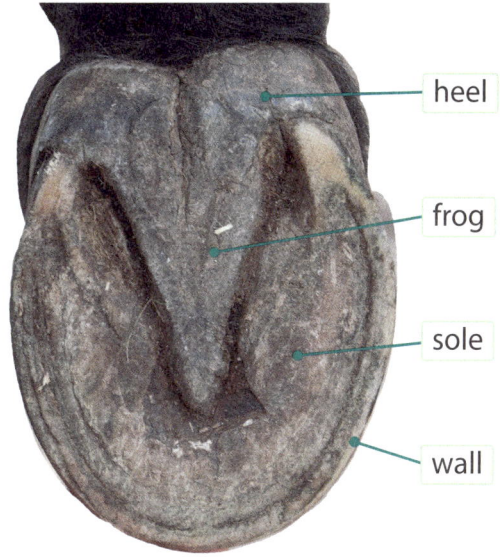

- heel
- frog
- sole
- wall

Fact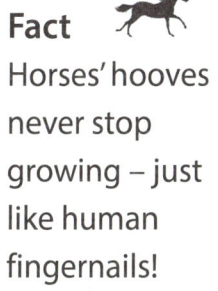
Horses' hooves never stop growing – just like human fingernails!

A farrier heats up the iron horseshoe to bend it into shape, then uses iron nails to attach it to the hoof.

Does that sound painful? It isn't! Horses' hooves are made of keratin, the same stuff as our fingernails and toenails, so it's almost like the farrier is giving the horse a pedicure. Horses actually hold out their hooves to help the farrier work.

Fact
Foals are born with soft coverings on their hooves called slippers. The slippers fall off after they're born.

The first king of Lesotho

About 200 years ago, the British and the Dutch travelled to South Africa and took the land belonging to the indigenous people. Moshoeshoe was a Sotho clan leader who wanted to protect his nation.

Moshoeshoe knew he needed more than just a safe location – he also needed horses for any possible battle. He started collecting as many horses as possible.

painting of Moshoeshoe I from the 19th century

Moshoeshoe eventually owned more horses than any other clan leader, and this made him even more successful in battle, because all his soldiers were mounted. Many South African clans wanted to fight for their independence and, when they joined Moshoeshoe, he gave their soldiers horses to ride too.

After years of fighting, Moshoeshoe made a deal with the United Kingdom to protect Lesotho. It became an independent country in 1966. Today, Moshoeshoe is called the father of Lesotho – and he couldn't have done it without the Basotho ponies.

Basotho ponies are so important, they appear on Lesotho's currency.

Bonus
Horses around the world

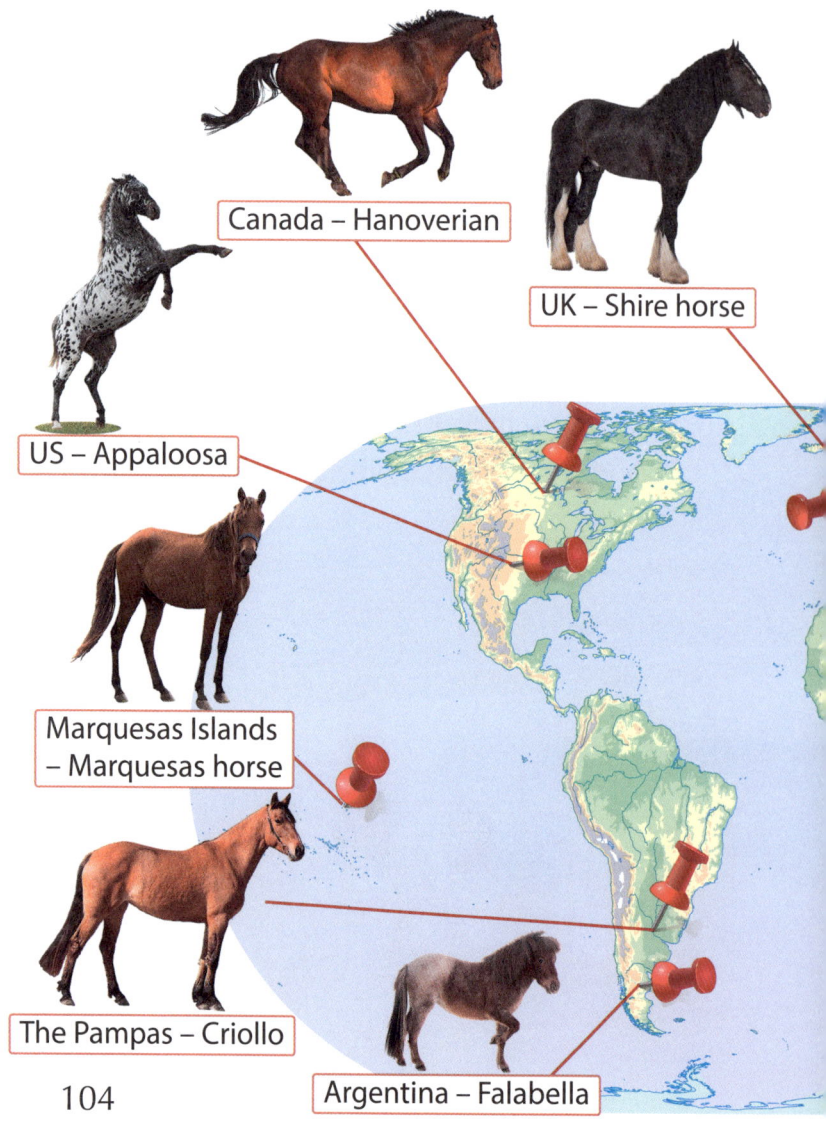

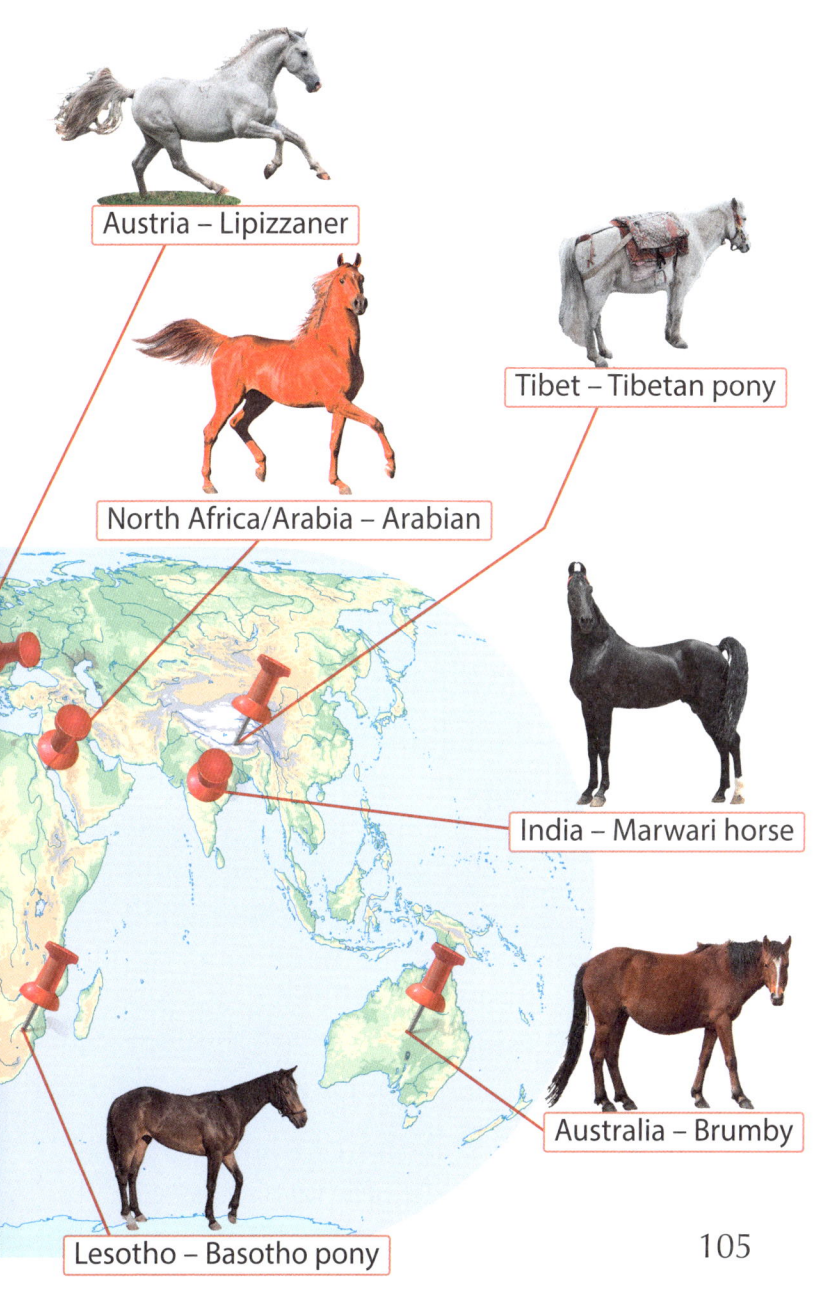

About the author

Have you always been an author?

I've always loved writing, so I always knew I wanted to be an author. For many years I did lots of different jobs and worked in all sorts of places: a bookshop, a hospital, even an airport! Finally my dream came true and I became a full-time writer.

Ella Foxglove

Did you already know lots about horses or did you have to do a lot of research for this book?

Horses are one of my favourite animals, so when I started writing this book, I thought it would be easy. It turns out there's a lot I didn't know about horses and I learned a lot along the way!

What did you learn while writing this book?

I learned that even though we now have modern technology that means we don't rely on horses as much as we used to, they still play important roles in societies around the world.

What do you hope readers get from your book?

I hope readers of my book enjoy learning about all the different horses around the world and appreciate the special relationship humans have with these amazing creatures. There are lots of places where you can meet horses for free and get to know them, like the Hook Norton Shire horses who visit local fairs to show off their intricate harnesses and horse brasses.

What's your favourite thing about writing?
I love discovering new stories while I write. When I was writing this book, I read books about the history of Australian stockwomen and was fascinated by their unique way of life and the challenges they faced. I also loved reading Aimé Tschiffely's book *The Ride* about his journey with his two Criollo horses Mancha and Gato. Aimé wrote his book a long time ago and uses old-fashioned language, but as a reader I could still feel the warmth he had for his horses and the depth of their bond.

Why did you want to write this book?
As a child I rode a chestnut pony named Foxglove, and when I grew up and became a writer, I decided to name myself after her. Foxglove was clever, curious, and a bit cheeky, and I'll never forget the bond we shared. Writing a book about horses was a way to share my love for these amazing animals.

Do you have a favourite horse or fact in the book?
My favourite horses are the Hook Norton Shire horses, because when I was growing up my family often visited the Heavy Horse Farm Park in Dorset to meet the Shire horses there. I also love the story of Lord and Lady Fisher, because I found out my mum visited their wildlife park in the 1970s and met the Falabellas! She was able to tell me how excited everyone was to meet such unique miniature horses.

What would you like to write about next?
My other favourite animal is the fox, and just like horses, there are all different kinds of foxes all over the world. I'd love to write about different fox species and their unique traits, like Arctic foxes who live alongside polar bears, or grey foxes who can climb trees.

Book chat

What did you know about horses before reading this book?

What have you learned from this book?

Have you ever seen or ridden a horse?

What horse would you most like to meet?

Which was your favourite horse?

Do you have a favourite fact from the book?

Did anything in this book surprise you?

Do you have a favourite photo? Why do you like it?

If you had to give the book a new title, what would you choose?

If you could ask the author anything, what would you ask?

If you were to write a non-fiction book about an animal, which animal would you choose to write about and why?

Who would you recommend this book to and why?

Which horse from the book would you most like to ride (or not like to ride) and why?

Are there any horse breeds in the book you'd heard of before?

Are there any horse breeds in the book you'd never heard of?

What was the most surprising thing you learned while reading?

Have you ever seen a working horse?

Book challenge:

Next time you see a horse in real life, on TV or in a book, see if you can identify any of its markings.

Collins
BIG CAT

Published by Collins
An imprint of HarperCollins*Publishers*

The News Building
1 London Bridge Street
London
SE1 9GF
UK

Macken House
39/40 Mayor Street Upper
Dublin 1
D01 C9W8
Ireland

Text © Danielle Coombs 2025
Design and illustrations © HarperCollins*Publishers* Limited 2025

Danielle Coombs asserts her moral right to be identified as the author of this work.

10 9 8 7 6 5 4 3 2 1

ISBN 978-0-00-876794-5

All rights reserved. No part of this publication may be reproduced, stored in a retrieval system, or transmitted in any form by any means, electronic, mechanical, photocopying, recording or otherwise, without the prior written permission of the Publisher or a licence permitting restricted copying in the United Kingdom issued by the Copyright Licensing Agency Ltd, 5th Floor, Shackleton House, 4 Battle Bridge Lane, London SE1 2HX.

Without limiting the exclusive rights of any author, contributor or the publisher of this publication, any unauthorised use of this publication to train generative artificial intelligence (AI) technologies is expressly prohibited. HarperCollins also exercise their rights under Article 4(3) of the Digital Single Market Directive 2019/790 and expressly reserve this publication from the text and data mining exception.

British Library Cataloguing-in-Publication Data
A catalogue record for this publication is available from the British Library.

Download the teaching notes and word cards to accompany this book at:
http://littlewandle.org.uk/signupfluency/

Get the latest Collins Big Cat news at
collins.co.uk/collinsbigcat

Author: Ella Foxglove
Illustrator (pg 77): Doris Shermadhi (Astound US)
Publisher: Laura White
Product manager and commissioning editor: Caroline Gre
Series editor: Charlotte Raby
Development editor: Catherine Baker
Project manager: Emily Hooton
Copyeditor: Sally Byford
Proofreader: Catherine Dakin
Cover designer: Sarah Finan
Typesetter: 2Hoots Publishing Services Ltd
Production controller: Sophie Waeland
Printed in the UK.

This book contains FSC™ certified paper and other controlled sources to ensure responsible forest management.

For more information visit: www.harpercollins.co.uk/green

Made with responsibly sourced paper and vegetable ink

Scan to see how we are reducing our environmental impact.

Acknowledgements
The publishers gratefully acknowledge the permission granted to reproduce the copyright material in this book. Every effort has been made to trace copyright holders and to obtain their permission for the use of copyright material. The publishers will gladly receive any information enabling them to rectify any error or omission at the fi opportunity.

Front cover Pawel Uchorczak/Shutterstock, p8 Realimage/Alamy, p9 afin/Alamy, p10b reppans/Alamy, p11 Sheila McCarron/Alamy, p12 David McGill/Alamy, p13 Neil McAllister/Alamy, p15tr Tierfotoagentur/Alamy, p16 Anadolu/Getty Images, p17(all) Mark Pain/Alamy, p18 Associated Press/Alamy, p19tl APA-PictureDesk/Alamy, p19tr Associated Press/Alamy, p19b Jack Taylor/Getty Images, p20 imageBROKER.com/Alamy, p21 ullstein bild Dtl/Getty Images, p22tr Marc Tielemans/Alamy, p23 Joe Blossom/Alamy, p25 Juniors Bildarchiv GmbH/Alamy, p26 Metropolitan Museum of Art/Public Domain, p29t unknown author/Public Domain, p29b Juniors Bildarchiv GmbH/Alamy, p31 Tom Salyer/Alamy, p34 LIU JIN/Getty Images, p35t Alison Wright/Getty Images, p36 Pictures Now/Alamy, p38br Sari O'Neal/Alamy, p45t Tierfotoagentur/Alamy, p46t Leon Werdinger/Alamy, p46b John McAnulty/Alamy, p49t Life on white/Alamy, p51 Lars Hagberg/Getty Images, p52t Associated Press Alamy, p52b & 55tr Imago/Alamy, p55b Ariadne Van Zandbergen/Alamy, p60 & 61 Popperfoto/Getty Images, p64tl Juniors Bildarchiv GmbH/Alamy, p65 VW Pics/Getty Images, p67 Christopher Pillitz/Getty Images, p68t & 69 Schweizer Familie/Public Domain, p71 Juniors Bildarchiv GmbH/Alamy, p72tr Inge Johnsson/Alamy, p72b Henry Arden/Getty Images, p73tl roger tillberg/Alamy, p73bl Christ Webb/Alamy, p75 Chronicle/Alamy, p78 P.j.Hickox/Alamy, p80b Selfwood/Alamy, p82l Connect Images/Alamy, p83t Sylvain Lefevre, Getty Images, p83b Hemis/Alamy, p85t Photo Josse/Leemage/Getty Images, p85br Greg Balfour Evans/Alamy, p87 Hemis/Alamy, p88 Aldona Griskeviciene/Alamy, p89 Aldona Griskeviciene/Alamy, p91 & 92 Marialtina/Alamy, p94 Jacques-Louis David/Kunsthistorisches Museum/Public Domain, p95t Nick-D/CC-BY-SA-3.0, p97 Gooreen collection/Public Domain, p98l & 100 Marco Longari/Getty Images, p102 Natal Archives, Pietermaritzburg, South Africa/Public Domain p104c Connect Images/Alamy, p104bl Juniors Bildarchiv GmbH/Alamy, p105bl Marco Longari/Getty Images. All other photos – Shutterstock.